3 8538 00001 1838

W9-BWJ-845

Limpy's Homemade Sausage
. . . and then some
For the Hunter and the Homemaker

S.G. Pierce

Acknowledgements

Many thanks to the following people, for without them this project could not have gotten off of the ground!

—S.G.Pierce

Consulting, recipes, and photographs..Limpy
Word processing, computer operations..Jeff Whitehair
Graphic Design..Ronald Wolf

Many thanks to all of the wild game hunters of the armed forces, both retired and in active duty, from San Diego to Vandenberg Air Force Base.

—Limpy

© 1998 S.G. Pierce
ALL RIGHTS RESERVED. No part of this book may be reproduced in any means without the written consent of the Publisher, except in the case of brief excerpts in critical reviews and articles.

Published in 1998 by:
Frank Amato Publications, Inc.
PO Box 82112 • Portland, Oregon 97282 • (503) 653-8108

Softbound ISBN: 1-57188-170-0 Softbound UPC: 0-66066-00368-3

Preface

Limpy, like many in this country, comes from a long line of hunters on both sides of his family. Starting out as a lad getting pointers from Dad and Grandpa, he continued his love for the outdoors well into adulthood, which led to a profession that nowadays is almost obsolete.

Limpy is a retired meat cutter who apprenticed under a Danish head meat cutter from the old school in Denmark. He has worked for custom slaughterers, retail meat markets and grocery stores during his thirty years at this profession.

Due to a leg injury he could no longer ignore, Limpy concentrated his talents exclusively on sausage making and the smoking of all meats and poultry for his family and friends.

The recipes in this book are all fine–tuned, with a lot of family favorites added to complete anybody's homemade feast.

Limpy is well aware that everyone's taste buds differ. Some like their meats hot and spicy, while others like them on the mildly–spiced side. Some prefer lots of garlic and/or onion in their food, while others would prefer their own particular balance of these flavorings. Limpy is always altering recipes that he finds in cookbooks, and is always frustrated at having no place to write down his own ideas and variations. After you have followed a recipe in this book which doesn't quite fit your particular "buds," you can use the "notes" column in the left margin of each page to write in any differences in ingredients or in measurements of spices, until you have it just the way you like.

I invite your questions and feedback. If you would like to contact me, you can reach me by mail at the following address:

S.G. Pierce
1305 North H Street
Suite A #141
Lompoc, CA 93436
FAX: (805)737-0346

E-mail: peach.tree@calbbs.com

May you enjoy these recipes on your bar–b–que and dinner tables for many years to come!

S.G. Pierce, June 1998

Table of Contents

Table of measurements

Lbs. = Pounds   gal. = Gallons
C. = Cups   qt. = Quarts
Tb. = Tablespoons   pt. = Pints
tsp. = teaspoons   floz. = Fluid Ounces

The quantities listed in each horizontal row are equivalent to each other

Lbs.	C.	Tb.	tsp.	gal.	qt.	pt.	floz.
1						1	
	1	16					8
	$^3/_4$	12					6
	$^2/_3$	$10^2/_3$					$5^1/_3$
	$^1/_2$	8					4
	$^1/_3$	$5^1/_3$					$2^2/_3$
	$^1/_4$	4					2
	$^1/_8$	2					1
		1	3				
	16			1	4	8	128
	8			$^1/_2$	2	4	64
	4			$^1/_4$	1	2	32
	2				$^1/_2$	1	16
	1				$^1/_4$	$^1/_2$	8

Glossary of meat smoking and preparation terms and procedures

Many of the recipes in this book will refer to certain words and procedures that you will need to have a good understanding of in order to perform the task successfully. When you arrive at a recipe that contains a word or a procedure that you don't fully understand, refer back to this glossary for documentation. Photographs appear throughout the book.

Bacon Hangers
Six or eight–pronged hooks that are used to hang the bacons in the smoker. One end penetrates the bacon end, with the other end draped over the smoke sticks in the smoker. To smoke bacon, see recipe on page 19.

Smoked bacons on bacon hangers

Bacon hangers and net hooks

Brine
A solution made of salt, sugar, water, and prague powder used to cure hams and bacon. For more information on prague powder see page 24. For brine recipes to be used with various meats see pages 19–20.

Brine pump
A large hypodermic–type needle and syringe (with about a 4oz. capacity) used to inject the brine solution into the meat at various points in order to cure. See photograph on page 61.

Boning knife
A sharp knife with a 5 or 6–inch long blade used to cut along the bone in meats.

Burner
The burner (which can be gas or electric) is placed at the bottom of the smoker to regulate the internal smoker temperature. See page 16 for more information.

Casings

Sausage casings are of three types: natural, synthetic (fibrous), or collagen.

(a) Natural casings are made from the intestines of the lamb, hog or beef. Keep refrigerated.

(b) Synthetic casings need not be refrigerated. Soak the amount needed in water for a short while. Shake off excess water, then use. You know it as the covering you peel away from salami before you eat it.

(c) Collagen casings are run through water inside and out before use, and unlike synthetic, they are edible. See pages 25–26 for more information about casings.

• When you work with natural casings, especially hog casings, you will run into ones that split as you are stuffing them. Cut them with a sharp knife at the split and tie off the end. Any sausage mixture that is exposed can be put back into the stuffer and stuffed again. Be sure to tie off the other end also, before you put the casing back onto the stuffer tube.

• When the casings are completely stuffed and you go to twist into links, try to make them come out in an even number. They will hang better on the smoke sticks that way.

• Fibrous casings (synthetic) can't be twisted into links. Both ends need to be tied off with butcher twine. Limpy suggests using synthetic casings that come with one end pre–tied. Not only is one end tied tighter than you yourself can tie them, but also they come with a built–in hanging loop for your smoke sticks (see page 56).

Damper

A turnable flap in the smoker pipe used to control the amount of released smoke from the chips or sawdust. Many recipes will call for you to dry the sausage with the damper completely open, and then close it $1/4$ turn as you raise the smoker temperature to smoke. The damper is usually located about $1/3$ to $1/2$ the way up the smoke pipe.

Fermento

A fermented dairy product in powder form that adds that zing to beef sticks (Slim Jims).

Gamble

A steel rod that turns up at each end. It is used to raise the animal that you are about to skin and split off of the ground. It is inserted through the Achilles tendon of each hind leg of your animal. See the section on field dressing your game on pages 21–23.

Grinder and grinding plate

The grinder, or meat chopper, is used to grind the meat. Cut meat into usable chunks before adding it to the grinder. The grinding plate has holes in it that the meat is squeezed through. The size of the holes determines the coarseness of the ground meat. See page 17.

Ham nets and net hooks

Nylon or twine–made nets used to contain hams (singly) so that they can be hung inside the smoker. Use a net hook (an S–shaped hook), by hooking one end through the net, and the other end around the smoke stick. See photos, page 8 (net hooks) and 69 (netting).

Lugger

A large, heavy plastic container which holds large amounts of sausage or meat, making it easier to transport your product from here to there (see photo on page 72).

Measurement of meat

Stated weights are the net weight of the meat after the bone and excess fat are removed.

Smoker

The smoker is basically the oven that is used to cook your sausages. It is an enclosed container with burners at the bottom, which are used to raise the internal smoker temperature high enough to cook the meat. Sawdust, or "smoke" is placed in a stainless steel or cast iron pan and put on one of the burners, in order to add the desired smoky flavor and color. See the section which deals specifically with smoke later for a more detailed description. First–time smokers or beginners can purchase small electric smokers at hardware or sporting goods stores (see the references on page 83). You won't be able to smoke in large quantities, but eventually you can get something bigger. You can also build your smoker yourself (see pages 15–16 for information).

Smoke

Limpy likes to use dry smoke (it resembles sawdust) for smoking sausage because it gives the finished product a nice shiny color and a mild smoky flavor. It's more costly, however. Damp smoke lasts longer because it takes longer to burn. Limpy uses damp smoke when he smokes hams, bacon, and poultry. Hickory chips, apple, cherry, alder etc. are easy to purchase from catalogs or hardware stores. Also, you can usually find them in the bar–b–que section of the store. They come in bags that are filled with what resembles sawdust. You will need to experiment with the different flavors they come in until you find the one that's right for your taste buds. Place about $1^1/2$ cups of chips or sawdust in a 6" or 8" stainless steel pan that will go on top of your burner that is in your smoker. Using a stainless steel (or cast iron) pan is important. Anything else would melt under high heat. If the recipe calls for damp smoke, add a little water to the chips or sawdust until they are damp but *not* wet or soaked. Recipes in this book will tell you when to add the smoke.

Smoke continued...

- When filling your pan with "smoke" for the smoker, be generous. Use 1¹/₂ C. at the very least.

- The pan of smoke will last for one "smoking."

- After smoking your favorite recipe, be very careful with the sawdust or chips residue that is leftover in your pan. You'd be surprised at how hot that residue is. When the time comes to dispose of it, make sure that it has completely cooled.

Smoke sticks

Smoke sticks are used to hang the stuffed sausages and whole meats inside of the smoker while they cook. Netted hams and bacons are hung by hooks that are set on the smoke stick, which looks like a broom handle. Sausage links are looped around the stick. The smoke sticks can be made of stainless steel, also. The smoke sticks are fastened to the inside of the smoker walls by brackets. See page 15 for information on attaching support brackets inside of your smoker.

Stuffer

Your ground sausage or salami is stuffed into a casing (either natural or synthetic, depending upon the recipe) by means of a sausage stuffer. The sausage stuffer is a cannister with a tube that the ground meat exits from at the bottom, and a crank and flat piston that pulses the meat down from the top as you crank (see the photo on page 31). The meat is pulsed through the tube and into the casing. First, slip one end of the casing over the end of the tube. Then, tie the other end of the casing into a knot. In order to prevent the casing from slipping off, hold the casing onto the tube with your left hand while cranking with the right hand. As the meat makes its way into the tube and then into the casing, give the casing some slack, but still hold it onto the tube. When you have entirely filled the casing with the ground meat, remove the casing from the tube and tie the end of it into a knot so that the meat can't leak out. After your meat is in the casing and both ends are tied off, follow the casing down to a desired length (about 6" or as indicated by the recipe), pinch gently and twist the link three or four times like you would if you were making a balloon animal. You can also use butcher twine to tie the links if you wish. Be careful not to fill the casings too tightly, or they will burst. There are many varieties of stuffers that you can purchase at specialty shops or through mail order catalogs, but the crank method is best due to the control that it gives the user. If you own a Kitchen Aid (see the photo on page 33), you can purchase a sausage stuffer attachment for it. Some grinders have a sausage stuffer attachment that you can use after you grind the meat.

A pictorial overview of the sausage making process

**Ground meat in bowl
ready to stuff**

**Put mixture into stuffer
cannister**

**Slide the sausage casing
onto the tube**

**Crank handle - pulses
the meat into casing**

**Hold the casing to help
guide while stuffing**

**Tie into links with twine
as an option to twisting
into links**

> "This book is written for the frustrated hunter and backyard butcher"

N o t e s

....
....
....
....
....
....
....
....
....
....
....
....
....
....
....
....
....
....
....
....
....
....
....
....

Introduction...

This book is written for the frustrated hunter and backyard butcher, who eventually has to come to grips with reality. Once his game is down, dressed and skinned, the questions arise, "Who do I take it to?" And "Am I going to get *all* of my meat back?" The only solution is to do it yourself.

Even if you don't hunt...

Even if you don't hunt, and want to make sausage, salami, smoked hams and bacon, it's very easy and affordable to do, through cuts of meat purchased at your local grocery store. Spices, casings, ham nets, grinders, stuffers, are easily obtained through butcher supply stores and meat markets. Your older meat cutters would be very helpful, since they've had to break beef in the past, and know all the ins and outs of this lost trade of meat cutting.

30 years of experience...

Being a retired meat cutter and sausage maker, Limpy has compiled 30 years of experience, and I'm passing along his knowledge in this book of easy, no–hassle tips and recipes, including ham and bacon smoking, turkey and fish. The best thing about this hobby is, you can always eat your mistakes!

Important things to remember...

1) Cleanliness is a must.
2) Keep your meat cold, and under refrigeration until you start to grind.
3) Weigh spices, wash casings, sterilize the grinder head, stuffer & tubes with scalding water before using grinding knives and plates.
4) Use a good grade of salt, Kosher or non–iodized.
5) Have everything ready to go and laid out before you grind your meat.

"The best thing about this hobby is, you can always eat your mistakes!"

N o t e s

....
....
....
....
....
....
....
....
....
....
....
....
....
....
....
....
....
....
....
....
....
....
....
....
....
....
....
....

This is an easy–to–follow, well rounded, "basic" book of sausage making and meat smoking. Included are some of Limpy's favorite, tasty, and easy–to–follow recipes. To make your meals complete, I have also included recipes of foods and toppings to accompany the sausages and other meats, such as beans, pizza and breads, sauces, relish and salsa.

Kitchen items you will need...

1) Nonfat powdered milk
2) Corn sugar
3) Fermento
4) Internal thermometer
5) Assorted bulk spices such as cayenne pepper, mace, coriander, marjoram, paprika, nutmeg, thyme, white pepper, cardamon, ginger, and garlic.

Other necessities...

Hand saw (25" market)
Boning knife and assorted sharp knives
Bacon hangers
Net hooks (for hams)
Sawdust
Stainless steel or cast iron pan
Smoke sticks
Stocking nets
Meat lugger and stainless steel bowls
5–gallon plastic pails
Plastic cutting boards (optional)
Liquid smoke (optional)
Butcher twine
Freezer paper
Meat grinder
Sausage stuffer with assorted tubes
Assorted casings (natural and synthetic)
Brine pump
Prague powder
Weight scale
Electric or gas smoker

> *"When building a
> meat smoker, use
> an ice storage box"*

N o t e s

....
....
....
....
....
....
....
....
....
....
....
....
....
....
....
....
....
....
....
....
....
....
....
....
....
....
....
....
....
....
....
....
....

Building a meat smoker...

When building a meat smoker, you can use an old refrigerator or an ice storage box. They are the same ice boxes that you see in the grocery store that they use to store block or crushed ice. Limpy found his at a junk yard. These work best because they are insulated. Make sure that they are steel–lined, not plastic. You don't want the plastic to melt. You can remove all the plastics from the inside yourself.

Attaching the pipe...

Cut a 4" diameter hole in the top center of the refrigerator. A 4" stove pipe, damper, and hooded top can be purchased at most hardware stores. Drill a hole through the pipe about 1 foot up and attach the damper. Attach the top of the hood to the pipe. Insert the completed pipe through the hole in the top of the smoker . With tin snips, cut and flange the bottom of the pipe. Make sure you caulk the flanged bottom before you screw the pipe to the inside top of the refrigerator. Caulk around the outside top of the refrigerator or ice box also, where the pipe fits through the hole.

Adding support brackets...

You will need brackets on both sides of the inside of your smoker, in order to rest your smoke sticks on. Use an angle iron for this. Space each bracket about 10"–12" apart, so that your sausage can hang without touching the sausage that hangs directly below it.

Monitoring the smoker temperature...

To keep track of the internal temperature inside your smoker, buy an 8" stem thermometer. Drill a hole, just large enough to insert the thermometer from the outside, through the box to the inside, about eye level. You will then always know how hot the inside of the smoker is without opening the door.

Gas is preferable to electricity for heat...

For the heat source, you should use gas instead of electricity. Gas is drier and you can smoke hotter with less chance of a fire. Electric hot plates will flare up and catch on fire at 165°. You can smoke at 180° – 200° with gas. You can use natural gas hooked up by your plumber, or propane. Limpy's burner is a gas camp stove with wrought iron legs that he picked up at a yard sale. You might be able to get one at a camping supply store or swap meet. Don't confuse this with a "Coleman" stove.

Monitoring the meat temperature...

An internal thermometer with a 4 foot or so lead, is a **must**. The probe can be inserted into the center of the meat you are smoking. The lead can be fed through the closed door or run down the smoke stack. With the thermometer sitting on top of your smoker, you can read the internal temperature of the meat without opening the door. The less the door has to be opened, the better. The probe with lead can be purchased through some of the butcher supply shops that are listed in the back of this book (page 83). *The Sausage Maker* also sells various kinds of small smokers and smoker accessories. Most references in the back of the book can send you catalogs.

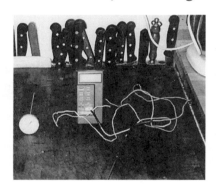

Internal thermometer with lead wire and probe

Front view of smoker

> ### "Pork is a good base to mix with any kind of meat"

N o t e s

....
....
....
....
....
....
....
....
....
....
....
....
....
....
....
....
....
....
....
....
....
....
....
....
....
....
....
....

Photo at right: Converted ice box used as a meat smoker, side view

A 4" pipe with a hooded top extends up from the inside of the smoker through a hole in the top

Different meats require using different–sized grinding plates...

Many sausage recipes call for the use of different–sized grinding plates. For example, you can use a $^1/_8$" plate for ground meat. A $^3/_{16}$" or a $^1/_4$" plate would be used to grind Italian sausage, and a $^3/_8$" to a $^5/_8$" plate is used to make Linguisa sausage. The beginner can easily get by with using just two plate sizes...a $^1/_8$" for ground meat and a $^3/_8$" for chili grind. Each plate alone is for two different purposes, but combine the use of two grinding plates in the same recipe, and you get the texture you need for Polish sausage. You would grind the lean meat with the $^3/_8$" plate, and the fatter meat with the $^1/_8$" plate. No matter which plate you use, homemade tastes better than store–bought any day. It's also healthier, especially since you know what's in it.

Do you want to know which kinds of beef, fowl, and pork to buy? Do you know which to use and when? The following tips contain answers to all of these questions.

Pork...

Pork is a good base to mix with any kind of meat. You can't go wrong mixing pork with beef, venison, turkey or ostrich. Pork added to this lean meat not only makes it easier to work with, but cuts the dryness and adds flavor to your finished product.

N o t e s

....
....
....
....
....
....
....
....
....
....
....
....
....
....
....
....
....
....
....
....
....
....
....
....
....
....
....
....
....
....
....
....
....

Beef...

Buy beef chuck, bone–in or boneless when on sale. Beef chuck makes the best ground hamburger and you can use the bones for broth to add later in sausages such as Danish, English Bangers & Liver. The broth freezes well also. Freeze in 2–cup baggies, which would be good for 10 Lbs. of sausage or added to stew or pot roasts. Beef chuck and pork are good to use for salami, hot dogs, and knockwurst at a ratio of 6 Lbs. beef to 4 Lbs. pork. When making beef/pork sausage recipes, be it breakfast, Polish, Italian etc. you can substitute venison for the beef part.

Chicken...

When making chicken sausage, use $1/2$ boneless, skinless breasts, and $1/2$ boneless, skinless thighs. The sausage stays lean but the thighs make the sausage moist and flavorful. When you use fowl of any kind, clean up thoroughly. Wash your knives, cutting surfaces, grinder and stuffers with hot soapy water to prevent salmonella.

Turkey...

Turkeys are a good buy all year. Buy the big ones (20–25 Lbs.). Cut it up like a chicken, leaving the breast whole. Separate the thighs and drumsticks. Limpy bakes the legs for burrito filling. Skin and bone the thighs and wings. You can add pork to make turkey Italian sausage. Before smoking, pump the breasts (see page 20 for brining instructions), which you can use for making sandwiches. With small turkeys, cut the brining solution in half. Make broth from the bones and skin to use later in sausage or soups.

Bacon...

Purchase only fresh pork bellies. They run about 10–12 Lbs. on the average. The larger the better. Smoke them with the skin on, and use the skin later to flavor homemade beans. Pork bellies should be 35°– 40° before

"When making sausages, you can substitute venison for the beef part"

N o t e s

....
....
....
....
....
....
....
....
....
....
....
....
....
....
....
....
....
....
....
....
....
....
....
....
....
....
....
....
....

pumping. Pump the bacon all around the sides with a brine pump. Pump 8–10% of the weight of the pork bellies with this solution (below) for 25 Lbs. of bellies.

BACON BRINE
10 qt. cold water
12 oz. sugar
8 oz. prague powder
1 Lb. salt
2 oz. liquid smoke (optional)

Lay bellies out flat and pump around all sides. Each needle puncture should be about 2" apart. Put bellies in a lugger, skin side down for 3–4 days. Smoke in a preheated smoker. Use a gas smoker so that you can smoke at a higher temperature (180°–200°). Add 2 pans of damp sawdust. Limpy uses hickory sawdust from Missouri. It is a real nice sawdust blend that is good for smoking Polish sausage and salami (apple and alder sawdust are used for smoking fish and poultry). Smoke over a period of 4–6 hours or so. The internal temperature of the bellies should reach 140°–145° in order to be considered done. Hang to cool, then refrigerate until the next day.

HAM BRINE
Pork legs and/or pork shoulder picnics equaling 25 Lbs. of meat.
10 qt. cold water (40°)
1 Lb. salt
12 oz. sugar (or mixture of $^1/_2$ sugar and $^1/_2$ brown sugar)
10 oz. prague powder

Make enough brine to cover the hams. Dissolve ingredients into water. Pump the cooled hams (35°–40°) with cooled brine (35°–40°) all along the bone, and all around the whole ham. Submerge in leftover brine for 4–5 days. Put into ham nets (tying the net tops into knots before hooking), then hang in a preheated smoker. Raise the temperature to 180°–200°. Smoke with 2 pans of damp sawdust until the internal ham temperature reaches 148°–152°. They are considered fully cooked at this point. Pull, hang, cool and refrigerate.

> *"With gas, you can smoke hotter than with electric"*

N o t e s

....
....
....
....
....
....
....
....
....
....
....
....
....
....
....
....
....
....
....
....
....
....
....
....
....

TURKEY BRINE
5 gal. water
$1^1/_4$ Lbs. sugar
$^1/_2$ Lb. brown sugar
$2^1/_4$ Lbs. salt
1 Lb. prague powder

Chill the turkey and brining solution to 38°– 40°. Clear the passage from inside the cavity to the neck, so the bird doesn't retain moisture. Pump the turkey with a brining needle all around various points of the bird. Put the turkey in a net to smoke. Submerge the turkey in the leftover brine you used to inject them with for 2–3 days. Smoke, using 2 pans of damp sawdust until the smoker temperature reaches 180°–200°. The internal temperature of the bird should reach 162°–165°, as with chickens, ducks, and geese. Keep refrigerated at all times after smoking is finished. Again, with gas you can smoke hotter. With electric, you can't. Higher temperatures might cause a fire, due to the fat dripping on the electric element.

Photo at right: Raw turkeys which have just been placed into the smoker

Photo at left: The finished product– turkeys smoked and hanging to cool before refrigeration

"Once dirt gets into the animal, it won't come out completely"

N o t e s

....
....
....
....
....
....
....
....
....
....
....
....
....
....
....
....
....
....
....
....
....
....
....
....
....
....
....
....
....

Field Dressing your game...

When field dressing your game (deer, pig, elk, etc.), roll it on it's back up next to a small shrub. Carefully make a small incision up the belly and remove the stomach, liver and intestine. Save the liver. Reach up further, going towards the upper body and puncture the diaphragm to release the blood. You can tilt the animal to make the blood flow easier. You can remove the lungs and the heart if you wish. If you do save the heart, put it and the liver back into the cavity for later.

With your knife, puncture some holes lengthwise on both sides of the incision. With string or twine (which you should always carry with you in your pack), sew the animal back up (with the liver and/or heart inside), including the bullet hole. This prevents dust, fox tails, and any foreign objects from getting inside of your animal. Once dirt and the like gets inside of your animal, it won't come out completely. This means that it will spread throughout the finished product when you cut and grind the meat.

Once the field dressing is completed, the game can be moved with confidence to a cleaner place, where the final steps can be taken. Don't forget to take photographs!

Hang your game by a gamble, by the hind legs. Split the aitch (pelvic) bone with a saw or sharp knife. Reach in and grab the bung. Get below the split aitch and loosen up towards the end. Start in front and cut around it's bung end. Reach in and pull the bung and bladder down and out. Be careful *not* to cut the bladder, but if you do, wash out the insides with vinegar and water. Use a clean towel to wipe out the inside. Split all the way down to the chin, then remove the wind pipe. Spread the rib cage and prop open the animal with a stick to keep the animal open so that air can circulate and cool it down faster. It's always best to clean the animal out with vinegar and water anyway.

> ***"Animals are easier to cut or bone when the meat has been aged properly"***

N o t e s

....
....
....
....
....
....
....
....
....
....
....
....
....
....
....
....
....
....
....
....
....
....
....
....
....
....
....
....
....
....
....

Some hunters skin the deer right away, and then hang it. Some leave the skin on and hang it up for 7–10 days. Skinning is easier if it is done right away, but the meat will dry out sooner. When you do skin your animal, start from the inside of the legs. Skin down each side of the incision that you made when you dressed the animal, to the inside of the front shanks, down to the chin. Skin around as far as you can. Finish the legs over the rump section to the tail. Pull the tail down and cut through the base to use as a handle when pulling down and skinning the back at the same time. Pull all the way down over the shoulders. The neck area is the hardest area to skin. Cut the head off and leave it attached to the skin.
Your carcass is now left to be split.

When breaking down your animal, split it in half, from the tail to the neck. Break the deer at the legs at the dimples on the lower back. Cut the shoulders straight across 2"–3" back from the arm pits and ***don't*** pull off the arm with the shoulder blade attached. That changes the shoulder from a nice workable chunk of meat into scraps for ground meat.

Don't forget to fry up your deer liver and/or heart that you saved during field dressing.

 Tip: Don't use the deer liver in the Smoked Liver Sausage recipe (page 55).

Hogs are a little different...

The shoulders are broken at the arm pits, and the legs are broken 2" or so above the aitch (pelvic) bone towards the lower rib section. Cut the ribs from the loin. Hogs don't need to age as long as a deer or an elk, 2–3 days are fine. Hang in a cooler or a cold place until firm. Animals are easier to cut or bone when the meat has been aged properly; 3–4 days for hogs, and 7–10 days for deer. Just remember to keep the animal as hair and dirt–free as possible for a tastier finished product.

> *"It pays to do a neat job of butchering and trimming"*

N o t e s

....
....
....
....
....
....
....
....
....
....
....
....
....
....
....
....
....
....
....
....
....
....
....
....
....
....
....
....
....
....
....
....
....
....

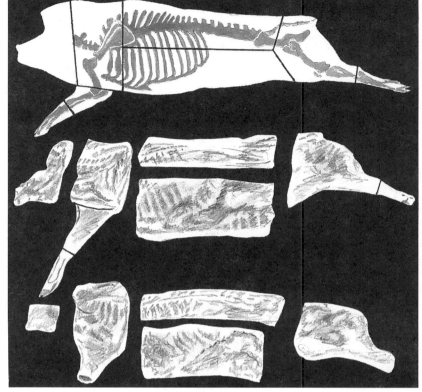

The Pork Carcass

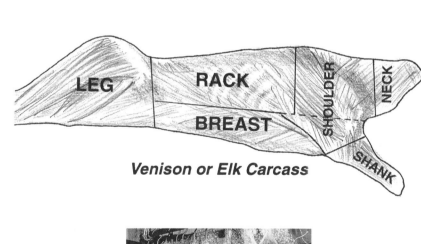

Venison or Elk Carcass

LEG · RACK · BREAST · SHOULDER · NECK · SHANK

Smoked Ham Hocks and Neck Bones

"Homemade tastes better than store–bought any day. It's also healthier, since you know what's in it"

N o t e s

....
....
....
....
....
....
....
....
....
....
....
....
....
....
....
....
....
....
....
....
....
....
....
....
....
....
....
....
....

Sausage making tips...

When Limpy comes across large pork shoulder butts, he cuts out the loin side that runs from the loin through the butt, and saves it for "poor mans Canadian bacon." The remainder is used for making sausage. Bacon brine is used for Canadian bacon (see page 19). Pump the meat, then soak it in brine for 3 days. Smoke the meat in netting until the internal temperature reaches 140°–145°. When using pork butts for sausage, remove the gland and blood spots from the meat. The gland is located in the back (fatter) portion of the butt. It is about the size of a large grape. After removing the excess fat, store the fat trimmings in the freezer in order to mix later with beef or venison ground meat. Limpy uses pork butts rather than shoulder picnics because they have less waste. Shoulders are cheaper, but they have skin, more bone, and contain more fat. The legs are too lean and dry for sausage.

Prague powder is a small amount of sodium nitrite mixed with salt. You order it pre–mixed. Use 2 tsp. prague powder to 10 Lbs. meat. Prague powder is used when smoking. Use 4 oz. per 100 Lbs. of meat with desired amounts of sugar and salt. For dry cured meats (pepperoni, Italian salami, etc.) use 12 oz. per 100 Lbs. of meat, with desired amount of sugar and salt.

Prague Powder

 Tip: Prague powder is for smoked or dried meats only, ***not*** to be used for fresh sausage

> *"When making sausage, prick the casings if an air pocket appears"*

N o t e s

....
....
....
....
....
....
....
....
....
....
....
....
....
....
....
....
....
....
....
....
....
....
....
....
....

When preparing sausage to smoke, use nonfat dry powdered milk in a ratio of 2 cups for every 10 Lbs. of meat. This works as a nice binder, with no added flavor. Add spices along with 2 cups of water to the powdered milk. When you finish smoking sausage or salami, run it under water for 15 minutes or so until cool to the touch (120° internal) so that the product won't shrink or wrinkle. When making salami, liver sausage and regular sausage, prick the casings if an air pocket appears. When cooking braunschwieger, knockwurst, hot dogs, bangers, or any precooked sausage, make sure that the water is no hotter than 165° or the casings may burst.

Notes on sausage casings...

Casing Type	Sizes (in mm)	Notes on Uses
Lamb (Natural)	22-24 24-26	Lamb casings are difficult to use, as they are very delicate and break easily.
Hog (Natural)	29-32, 32-35 35-38, 38-42	For small sausage. Separate & rinse in cold water inside & out. Freeze remaining casings in water in a baggie, either all or in smaller-sized packages for later use.
Fibrous (Synthetic)	2in-8in X 24in	Soak in water 5-10 min. Add a little vinegar & liquid smoke to prevent the meat from sticking.
Collagen	19	For Slim Jims (smoked sausage). Run through water at the time of stuffing.

Synthetic Casings

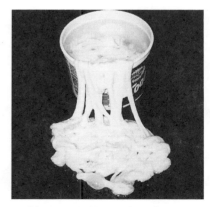

Natural Hog Casings

"Don't expect your first few batches to come out perfectly"

N o t e s

Photo at left: 8" synthetic casings for Bologna or large salami

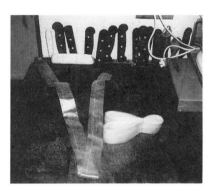

Photo at right: Collagen casings for use instead of natural casings

There are many more varieties of natural and synthetic casings on the market that you can order. Thirty years of hands on experience, and working with numerous professionals who brought their own special techniques and shortcuts to the business, is Limpy's main reference for this book. He has consumed many mistakes, so don't expect your first few batches to come out perfectly. You'll experience broken casings when stuffing too tight, or air pockets when stuffing too loose. An excellent reference and a complete source of supplies is obtainable through *South Bay Abrams Butcher Supply* in Huntington Beach, California. Specialty products like fermento (used in Slim Jims for that sour effect) can be purchased from *The Sausage Maker* in Buffalo N.Y. (See reference on page 83).

A note on spices...

Prepackaged spices for salami, sausage, etc., are readily available from catalogs, and are quick and easy to use. They usually season 25 Lbs. of meat. Limpy buys spices in large containers, or grinds his own in a coffee grinder (not used for coffee). Prepackaged spices are good to start with if you don't plan on making sausage often.

Cooked Sausage at a Glance				
Type	Spicy	Mild	Cooking Methods	Serving Suggestions
Bratwurst		X	Bar-B-Q, pan fry, broil, bake	In sandwiches, with red onions
Breakfast		X	Usually fried	Serve for breakfast with eggs
English Bangers		X	Pan fry, bake	Excellent for breakfast
Swedish Potato		X	Pan fry, bake, or broil	For breakfast, or in sandwiches
Italian	X		Bar-B-Q, broil, or pan fry	On pizza, spaghetti sauce, & lasagna
Danish		X	Boil	With potatoes, or with breakfast
Chicken Italian	X		Bar-B-Q, broil, or pan fry	Spaghetti sauce, pizza, sandwiches
Garlic		X	Broil or Bar-B-Q	Sandwiches, BBQ, or plain as is
Polish		X	Broil, bake, or Bar-B-Q	With steak or chicken
Chorizo	X		Pan fry	Beans, eggs, & with Mexican food
Linguisa	X		BBQ, broil, or slice & fry	Steak, all Bar-B-Q'ed foods
Kielbasa		X	Boil	Beans, macaroni & cheese, sandwiches
Slim Jims	X			Snacks, or wrap in tortilla
Andouille	X		Bar-B-Q or broil	Great in beans
Hot Links	X		Broil, boil, or Bar-B-Q	In hot dog buns or with any meal
Hot Dogs		X	Boil or Bar-B-Q	In buns with all of the toppings
Knockwurst		X	Boil	With potatoes or sauerkraut, buns
Bologna		X		Sandwiches, fried, w/cheese & crackers
Fire Sticks	X			Serve as you would Slim Jims
Pepperoni Sticks	X			Sandwiches, pizza, or plain as is
Beef Salami		X		In cubes for salads, or in sandwiches
Cotto Salami		X		Sandwiches, crackers & cheese, salads
Smoked liver		X		w/mayo for Paté, or sandwich spread
Venison Salami		X		Use as you would any salami
Venison Smokies		X	Broil or Bar-B-Q	Breakfast, or in sandwiches

Meat categories at a glance

Fresh Sausage

- Breakfast
- Bratwurst
- English Bangers
- Swedish Potato
- Garlic
- Italian
- Fresh Polish
- Danish
- Chorizo

Fowl

- Whole Turkeys
- Whole Chickens
- Whole Ducks
- Chicken Italian with Jalapeños and Sun–Dried Tomatoes

Pork

- Hams
- Bacon
- Canadian Bacon (from loin shoulder)

Smoked Sausage

- Polish
- Linguisa (semi-cooked)
- Hot Dogs
- Knockwurst
- Hot Links
- Andouille
- Dried Slim Jims
- Dried Spanish Chorizo Fire Sticks
- Bologna
- Cooked Salami
- Liver Sausage (Braunschweiger)
- Beef Salami

Venison

- Venison Smokies
- Venison Salami
- Venison breakfast sausage
- No haste Jerky

Fish

- Salmon
- Tuna
- Whole trout

Recipes

These sausage and salami recipes are in batches that yield 10 Lbs. The trim that you get off of a small hog or a small deer is equal to about 10 Lbs. of meat. If you are lucky enough to "get the big one" and you end up with more meat, adjust your spices accordingly. You get more trim when you bone your animal, as opposed to using a "butcher boy" band saw and cutting your animal with the bone in.

Once you go through the process a few times and taste the ultimate rewards of your own accomplishments, you will have a hard time buying store–bought sausage again. You'll see it in the store and proudly say to yourself, "I can make that!" Then you'll be hooked. Your sausage won't have the fillers and additives either.

Fresh Sausage

 To spice up your mild sausage, add one Tb. of cayenne pepper *or* two Tb. of crushed red chile to 10 Lbs. of meat

"Run cold water over sausages until cool to the touch to prevent shrinkage"

N o t e s

....
....
....
....
....
....
....
....
....
....
....
....
....
....
....
....
....
....
....
....
....
....
....
....
....
....
....
....

BRATWURST

10 Lbs. pork
1^1/$_2$ C. milk
^{1}/$_2$ C. chicken broth
3 eggs
2 C. nonfat powdered milk
1^1/$_2$ Tb. white pepper
1 Tb. mace
1 Tb. nutmeg
4 Tb. salt
1^1/$_2$ tsp. ginger
^{1}/$_2$ tsp. caraway seeds (optional)

Grind the meat through a ^{1}/$_8$" plate. Mix the meat well with the milk and then add all of the remaining ingredients and mix. Stuff the mixture into hog casings. You can leave it uncooked and store, or you can precook it by putting it into 165° water and cook until the internal temperature reaches 152°. Cool in cold running water until cold to the touch. You can then broil or cook it on the bar–b–que. If you want to smoke it, you need to add 2 tsp. prague powder when you're mixing the ingredients. Place in the smoker on smoke sticks. With the damper open, dry the links until they are dry to the touch. Close the damper ^{1}/$_4$ turn and raise the smoker temperature to 165°–175°. Add hickory or your favorite smoke. Smoke until the internal sausage temperature reaches 152°. Run cold water over the sausages until they are cool to the touch to prevent shrinkage. Store properly.

Sausage stuffer and tubes

> *"Always be sure your meat is clean of bone and glands"*

N o t e s

....
....
....
....
....
....
....
....
....
....
....
....
....
....
....
....
....
....
....
....
....
....
....
....
....
....
....
....
....
....
....
....
....
....

BREAKFAST or COUNTRY SAUSAGE

10 Lbs. pork
4 Tb. salt
$1^1/_2$ Tb. white pepper
$2^1/_2$ Tb. sage
1 Tb. nutmeg
1 Tb. thyme
$1^1/_2$ tsp. ginger
$^1/_2$ Tb. cayenne pepper
2 C. ice water

Trim the heavy fat off of the store–bought pork butts, or use the meat from your prized hog. If you are using the meat from your own game, always be sure that your meat is clean of bone and glands. For this recipe, Limpy likes to use the $^1/_8$" plate, grinding the meat only once.

To the ground meat, mix in the dry spices first. Then add the ice water. Mix all well. Bulk sausage is easiest for patties or you can use 22–24mm. lamb casings for the challenge of making link sausages. They cost about $25.00–$35.00 per hank and can stuff 55 Lbs. of meat. Wrap the finished product in freezer paper.

Wrap the finished product in freezer paper

N o t e s

....
....
....
....
....
....
....
....
....
....
....
....
....
....
....
....
....
....
....
....
....
....
....
....
....
....
....
....

ENGLISH BANGERS

10 Lbs. pork butts
5 Tb. salt
$1^{1}/_{2}$ Tb. white pepper
$1^{1}/_{2}$ tsp. ginger
$1^{1}/_{2}$ tsp. sage
$1^{1}/_{2}$ tsp. mace
$^{1}/_{4}$ tsp. coriander
$^{1}/_{2}$ C. bread crumbs
2 C. chicken broth
1 cup powdered milk

Grind the meat through a $^{1}/_{8}$" plate. Mix the meat well with the dry ingredients, then add the chicken broth. Mix thoroughly, then stuff the mixture into the hog casings. Twist or tie into links at $2^{1}/_{2}$ inches.

Freeze or save for the next meal. As an option, you can precook the sausages before storage by placing the links into 165° water until a temperature of 152° internally is reached.

Remove the links from the hot water and cool them off in cold running water. Dry, wrap and freeze.

Kitchen Aid grinder attachment

"You can bake, fry or boil to cook"

N o t e s

....
....
....
....
....
....
....
....
....
....
....
....
....
....
....
....
....
....
....
....
....
....
....
....
....
....
....
....
....
....
....
....
....
....
....
....

SWEDISH POTATO SAUSAGE

3 Lbs. lean boneless beef chuck
2 Lbs. lean pork
2 small onions
12 medium potatoes (peeled & cut up)
$1^1/_2$ tsp. black pepper
$1^1/_2$ tsp. white pepper
2 tsp. allspice
$^1/_2$ tsp. nutmeg
1 clove minced garlic
2 Tb. salt
2 cups powdered milk
2 cups water
1 tsp. sugar

Grind the meat, raw potatoes, and onions through a $^3/_8$" plate.

Mix together the dry ingredients, ground meat and water. Blend thoroughly. Then, re–grind the mixture through a $^3/_{16}$" or a $^1/_4$" plate.

Stuff the mixture into hog casings. You can bake, fry or boil to cook. Freeze as soon as possible, as this sausage is perishable.

Swedish Potato Sausage is a very bland sausage. It's often served with boiled or mashed potatoes, similar to a "New England" style dinner. After cooking, gravy can be made from the drippings by adding a little butter, milk, and flour. Spice up the gravy with a little white pepper and cayenne pepper (optional).

Tip:

- After stuffing the ground meat into the casings, if there are any air pockets you can prick them with a pin.

- Any excess sausage that you squeeze out when tying the casing end into a knot, can be added back into the stuffer canister.

> "Leave in a bulk
> state for use in
> lasagna or
> spaghetti"

N o t e s

....
....
....
....
....
....
....
....
....
....
....
....
....
....
....
....
....
....
....
....
....
....
....
....
....
....
....

ITALIAN SAUSAGE

10 Lbs. pork butts
$3^1/_2$ Tb. salt
$1^1/_2$ Tb. black pepper
2 Tb. fennel seed
$1^1/_2$ Tb. cayenne pepper
8 cloves minced garlic
1 Tb. paprika
$^1/_2$ tsp. marjoram
$^1/_2$ tsp. rosemary
$^1/_2$ tsp. thyme
1 cup Burgundy wine
1 cup water

Grind all of the meat through a $^3/_8$" plate for a coarser grind, or for a real nice texture, you can grind $^1/_2$ of the meat through a $^1/_8$" plate and the other $^1/_2$ of the meat through a $^3/_8$" plate.

Mix all of the ingredients until incorporated. Stuff the mixture into hog casings, or leave in a bulk state for use in lasagna or spaghetti. When it is linked in a casing, it is excellent on the bar–b–que.

If you don't like or can't have wine, you can omit it and use water instead. If this is the case, you will end up using 2 C. of water. If you want your sausage spicier, you can add 1–2 Tb. of crushed red chili.

Tip:

Italian sausage is also great smoked. Add 2 tsp. of prague powder and substitute water for the wine (making the total quantity of water 2 C.). Add 2 C. of nonfat powdered milk. Smoke as you would Polish Kielbasa (see the recipe on page 44).

> *"This sausage can also be precooked before storing"*

N o t e s

....
....
....
....
....
....
....
....
....
....
....
....
....
....
....
....
....
....
....
....
....
....
....
....
....
....
....
....
....
....

DANISH SAUSAGE

10 Lbs. pork butt
4 Tb. salt
½ tsp. allspice
1 Tb. white pepper
½ tsp. ground cloves
2 tsp. cardamon
1 tsp. ground coriander
1 cup nonfat powdered milk
1 large onion, minced fine
2 cups water or turkey broth

Grind the pork finely, through a $^1/_8$" plate.

Mix the dry ingredients together, then mix well with the pork. Incorporate either the water or the broth and mix well.

Stuff into hog casings. You can bake, broil, fry or bar–b–que this sausage.

If you prefer, this sausage can also be precooked before storing. Precook in a large pot of 165° water until the internal sausage temperature reaches 152°. Refrigerate or freeze.

Danish sausage is another mild but tasty sausage. If fried, it goes well served with your favorite potatoes. You can make gravy out of the drippings (see the recipe for Swedish Potato Sausage on page 34).

Tip: Some of these fresh sausage recipes call for precooking before storage. It is an option that you can try. Precooking, or boiling the sausage in water (where the internal sausage temperature reaches 152°–155°) gives the sausage a better color when you get around to serving it.

 "Twist or tie into **4"–5" links"**
N o t e s
· ·

CHICKEN ITALIAN SAUSAGE WITH SUN–DRIED TOMATOES AND JALAPEÑO CHILES

5 Lbs. boneless, skinless chicken thighs (fresh)
5 Lbs. boneless, skinless chicken breast (fresh)
$3^1/_2$ Tb. salt
$1^1/_2$ Tb. black pepper
2 Tb. fennel seed
$1^1/_2$ Tb. cayenne pepper
8 cloves garlic, chopped
1 Tb. paprika
3 Jalapeños, seeded & chopped
¼ C. chopped sun–dried tomatoes in olive oil
½ tsp. marjoram
½ tsp. rosemary
½ tsp. thyme
1 C. Burgundy wine
1 C. water
1 C. nonfat powdered milk

Grind the chicken through a $^3/_8$" grinder plate.

Mix together the tomatoes, garlic, and Jalapeños, then blend the mixture with the ground chicken. Add the remaining spices, then mix all together well. Add the water and wine, then blend all thoroughly.

Stuff the mixture into hog casings. Twist or tie into 4"–5" links. Refrigerate. This sausage is great for bar–b–que, or you can add it to spaghetti sauce. It also makes a great pizza topping.

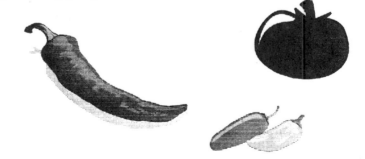

"Stuff into hog casings, then refrigerate"

N o t e s

....
....
....
....
....
....
....
....
....
....
....
....
....
....
....
....
....
....
....
....
....
....
....
....
....
....
....
....

GARLIC SAUSAGE

10 Lbs. pork
6 cloves chopped garlic
1 Tb. black pepper
1 Tb. sugar
6 Tb. salt
½ tsp. ground allspice
½ tsp. nutmeg
½ tsp. ginger
¼ tsp. cinnamon
½ tsp. thyme
1 C. white wine
1 C. water
1 C. nonfat powdered milk

Grind the meat through a $^3/_{16}$" plate.

Add all of the spices, along with the wine and water. Mix all together well.

Stuff the mixture into hog casings.

Link or tie at desired lengths, then refrigerate.

This sausage is great for bar–b–que.

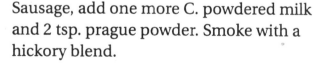

•If you would like to try to smoke the Garlic Sausage, add one more C. powdered milk and 2 tsp. prague powder. Smoke with a hickory blend.

•Garlic Sausage can be spiced up by adding 1½ Tb. cayenne pepper *or* 2 Tb. crushed red chile powder.

> *"If you are using a fatter pork, grind through a 1/8" plate"*

N o t e s

....
....
....
....
....
....
....
....
....
....
....
....
....
....
....
....
....
....
....
....
....
....
....
....
....
....
....
....

FRESH POLISH SAUSAGE

10 Lbs. boneless pork
5 Tb. salt
1 Tb. sugar
6 cloves garlic, chopped
1 tsp. paprika
$1/2$ tsp. white pepper
$1^1/2$ Tb. black pepper
1 tsp. cayenne pepper
2 tsp. marjoram
2 C. nonfat powdered milk
($1/2$ tsp. savory, optional)
2 C. ice water

Grind lean pork through a $3/8$" plate. If you are using a fatter pork, you can grind it through a $1/8$" plate.

Add the remaining ingredients to the ground meat, then stuff the mixture into hog casings. Link or tie into desired lengths. If you want to make meat patties, leave the meat in a bulk state.

Polish sausage is great on the bar-b-que, or you can broil it.

Fresh Polish sausage

> "Hog casings cost about $18.00–$20.00 per hank and can stuff about 110–120 Lbs. of meat"

N o t e s

....
....
....
....
....
....
....
....
....
....
....
....
....
....
....
....
....
....
....
....
....
....
....
....
....

CHORIZO

10 Lbs. pork butt
5 Tb. salt
1 C. water
1 C. white vinegar
6 Tb. paprika
2 Tb. cayenne pepper
6 Tb. chili powder
1 Tb. oregano
1 Tb. black pepper
10 cloves garlic, chopped finely
(or: 2 Tb. granulated garlic)
1 tsp. onion powder

Grind the meat through either a $1/8$" or a $1/16$" plate.

Mix the dry spices with the meat first, blending all together well. Incorporate the vinegar and water into the mixture.

Stuff the mixture into hog casings if you like, or if you're going to make meat patties, leave it in a bulk state. Hog casings cost about $18.00–$20.00 per hank and can stuff about 110–120 Lbs. of meat.

A spicy Mexican sausage, chorizo is great in eggs, beans or even on the bar–b–que.

• You can use a fatter pork in this recipe, because this sausage tends to dry out a little.

• Chorizo is best left in its bulk (ground) state. Usually, the only time you'll find it stuffed in casings is in the grocery store.

• This sausage is never smoked, unless it is the fire stick recipe (page 51).

Smoked Sausage

> **"Linguisa are ready to take out when they are firm to the touch"**

N o t e s

. . . .
. . . .
. . . .
. . . .
. . . .
. . . .
. . . .
. . . .
. . . .
. . . .
. . . .
. . . .
. . . .
. . . .
. . . .
. . . .
. . . .
. . . .
. . . .
. . . .
. . . .

LINGUISA (PORTUGUESE)

10 Lbs. pork on the fatter side
6 Tb. salt
2 tsp. prague powder
$1^1/_2$ Tb. sugar
2 Tb. black pepper
4 Tb. paprika
1 Tb. chili powder
1 Tb. cayenne pepper
1 Tb. marjoram
4 oz. red wine vinegar
2 C. ice water
2 C. powdered milk
10 cloves garlic, chopped
1 Tb. granulated garlic

Grind the meat through a $^3/_8$" or a $^5/_8$" plate, or cut the meat into small pieces. Mix the meat together with the spices, vinegar, water and garlic. Cover and let sit over night if you like. Stuff the mixture into hog casings, then twist off into 6"– 8" links. Onto smoke sticks, hang the sausages in the smoker with the vent open. Leave until they are dry to the touch. After they are dry, close the vent until $^1/_4$ closed, then raise the smoker temperature to 180°. Optionally, you can add $^1/_4$ pan of dry smoke for flavor. Linguisa are ready to take out when they are firm to the touch. Hang the sausages at room temperature until they are cool, then refrigerate. Linguisa is great served with steak, or with anything off of the bar–b–que.

Linguisa (semi–cooked)

> "Linguisa is great served with steak, or with anything off of the bar–B–Que"

N o t e s

....
....
....
....
....
....
....
....
....
....
....
....
....
....
....
....
....
....
....
....
....
....
....
....
....
....
....
....
....
....
....

LINGUISA HOT (15 Lb. batch)

15 Lbs. pork butt
8 Tb. salt
3 tsp. prague powder
2 Tb. black pepper
2 tsp. cumin
8 Tb. paprika
2 Tb. cayenne pepper
1 ball garlic
3 C. powdered milk
2 tsp. coriander
4 oz. wine vinegar
3 C. water

Prepare, cook, and serve in the same manner as the Linguisa recipe on the opposite page.

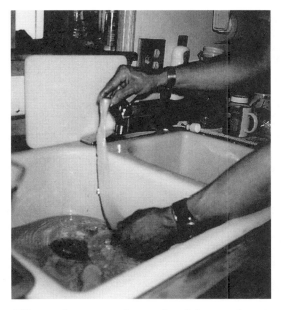

Rinse hog casings inside and out before stuffing with ground meat

N o t e s

....
....
....
....
....
....
....
....
....
....
....
....
....
....
....
....
....
....
....
....
....
....
....
....
....
....
....

SMOKED POLISH KIELBASA

10 Lbs. pork butt
2 tsp. prague powder
5 Tb. salt
1 1/2 Tb. black pepper
1 Tb. sugar
2 tsp. marjoram
1 tsp. paprika
6–8 cloves garlic, chopped
2 C. powdered milk
(1 tsp. savory optional)
2 C. cold water

Grind lean meat through a 3/8" plate. If you are using a fatter meat, grind through a 1/8" plate. Make sure the fatter meat doesn't have an excess of heavy fat on it. Trim the fat down to a happy medium. Remove all of the glands and blood clots.

Mix together the dry ingredients, and then blend together with the meat. Stuff the mixture into hog casings.

In the smoker with the damper wide open, hang the sausages until they are dry to the touch. Add damp smoke.

Close the damper until it is 1/4 of the way closed. Raise the heat until the smoker internal temperature reaches 180°. Smoke until the sausages reach an internal temperature of 152°.

Remove the sausages, cool them under cold water, let them dry and then refrigerate.

 Tip:
Limpy has dual burners inside of his smoker. With one side turned all the way up, it shouldn't exceed 180° inside of the smoker.

"Twist into links of desired length, about 10" or so"

N o t e s

. . . .
. . . .
. . . .
. . . .
. . . .
. . . .
. . . .
. . . .
. . . .
. . . .
. . . .
. . . .
. . . .
. . . .
. . . .
. . . .
. . . .
. . . .
. . . .
. . . .
. . . .
. . . .
. . . .
. . . .
. . . .
. . . .

SLIM JIMS

10 Lbs. beef or pork (or both in any mixture ratio)
6 Tb. salt
6 Tb. paprika
1 C. fermento
$^1/_2$ tsp. chile powder
1 Tb. cayenne pepper
1 tsp. crushed red chile
1 Tb. black pepper
1 tsp. white pepper
2 tsp. prague powder
$^1/_2$ tsp. ground celery (optional)
$^3/_4$ Tb. mace
2 Tb. granulated garlic
1 Tb. sugar
2 Tb. ground mustard

Grind the meat through either a $^3/_{16}$" or through a $^1/_8$" plate. Mix all of the dry ingredients together, then add them to the meat. Blend all together thoroughly. Stuff the mixture into 19mm. smoked collagen casings (you can also use small hog casings). Twist into links of desired length, about 10" or so.

Place the sausages into a smoker that is preheated to about 140°. Leaving the damper open, smoke for about 2 hours. Then, raise the smoker temperature to 180° (with-out closing the damper), until the internal temperature of the sausages reaches 150°. Hang the sausages until they have cooled, then refrigerate.

Slim Jims

"Hang the sausages in the preheated smoker for one hour until they are dry"

N o t e s

....
....
....
....
....
....
....
....
....
....
....
....
....
....
....
....
....
....
....
....
....
....

ANDOUILLE SAUSAGE

10 Lbs. pork butt
5 Tb. salt
2 Tb. black pepper
2 Tb. cayenne pepper
2 Tb. paprika
2 Tb. thyme
½ C. chopped garlic
1 Tb. sugar
2 tsp. prague powder
½ tsp. mace
2 C. nonfat powdered milk
2 C. water

Grind lean meat through a ¹/₄" plate. If you are using a fatter meat, grind it through a ¹/₈" plate.

Mix together the spices, water, etc. and blend all with the meat until completely incorporated. Stuff the mixture into hog casings.

Preheat the smoker to a temperature of 130°. With the damper fully open, hang the sausages in the preheated smoker for one hour until they are dry.

When the sausages have dried, close the damper until it is ¹/₄ of the way closed.

Add damp smoke, then raise the temperature of the smoker until it reaches 165°–170°. Smoke the sausages until their internal temperature reaches 152°.

Remove the sausages from the smoker, and cool down with running water. Hang them to dry, then refrigerate.

Some of these recipes will give you the option of pulling the sausages out of the smoker early (at 135°) to finish cooking in 165° water until the sausages reach 152° internally. Doing this gives the sausage a better visual appearance. Try it both ways, and see which you prefer.

> ***"Run the mixture through a food processor to emulsify"***

N o t e s

....
....
....
....
....
....
....
....
....
....
....
....
....
....
....
....
....
....
....
....
....
....
....
....
....
....
....

HOT LINKS

5 Lbs. beef chuck
5 Lbs. pork butt
4 tsp. chopped garlic
2½ Tb. cayenne pepper
1 Tb. black pepper
2 C. water
1 Tb. white pepper
2 C. nonfat powdered milk
4 Tb. salt
1 tsp. ground bay leaf
4 Tb. paprika
1 tsp. sugar
2 tsp. prague powder

Grind the meat through a $^3/_{16}$" plate. Add all of the ingredients to the meat. Mix all together well, then run the mixture through a food processor to emulsify.

Stuff the mixture into hog casings. Preheat the smoker to a temperature of 130°. With the damper fully open, hang the sausages in the preheated smoker for one hour until they are dry. When the sausages have dried, close the damper until it is $^1/_4$ of the way closed. Add damp smoke, then raise the temperature of the smoker until it reaches 165°–170°. Smoke the sausage links until their internal temperature reaches 152°. Rinse the sausages under cold running water until they are cool to the touch.

Alternatively, you can pull the links out of the smoker at 135° and place them in 165° water until the 152° temp-erature is reached. Remove the sausages and rinse them in cold water until they are cool, then refrigerate.

Tip:

- If a coarser sausage is desired, try grinding the meat through a $^1/_4$" plate.

- When adding the prague powder, Limpy likes to whisk it into the liquid, so that it dissolves and incorporates more evenly.

> "The lamb casings are pretty tough to get the hang of at first"

N o t e s

....
....
....
....
....
....
....
....
....
....
....
....
....
....
....
....
....
....
....
....
....
....
....
....
....

HOT DOGS

6 Lbs. beef chuck
4 Lbs. lean pork
6 Tb. salt
3 Tb. sugar
2 tsp. prague powder
1 tsp. dry mustard
3 Tb. white pepper
2 tsp. mace
1 tsp. allspice
1 tsp. coriander
1 Tb. paprika
1 Tb. garlic powder
2 C. powdered milk
2 C. water

Grind the meat through a $1/4$" plate.

Mix together the spices, water, and dry milk. Blend this mixture together with the ground meat. Re–grind the mixture through a $1/8$" plate. A more preferred method would be to run the mixture through a food processor to emulsify, adding water a little at a time until achieving a smooth blend.

Stuff the mixture into 24–26mm. lamb casings. The lamb casings are pretty tough to get the hang of at first. Hang the hot dogs on sticks in the smoker. Dry them for one hour with the damper open. Add $1/2$ pan of dry smoke, then raise the internal smoker temperature to 180°.

Smoke the hot dogs for one hour, or until the dogs reach about 135° internally. Remove them from the smoker, then cook in 165° water until they reach 152° internally. (Make sure that you have the water already heated and ready to go when you need it). Cool them in water. These dogs will have the snap when you bite into them!

 Tip: Use hog casings instead of lamb casings if $1/4$ Lb. dogs are desired

"Tie them into about 2" lengths with twine"

N o t e s

....
....
....
....
....
....
....
....
....
....
....
....
....
....
....
....
....
....
....
....
....
....
....
....
....
....
....
....
....
....

KNOCKWURST

6 Lbs. beef
4 Lbs. pork
2 C. powdered milk
6 Tb. salt
1 tsp. dry mustard
2 Tb. sugar
2 tsp. prague powder
4 Tb. white pepper
2 tsp. mace
½ tsp. allspice
1 tsp. coriander
1 Tb. garlic powder
2 Tb. paprika
2 cups cold water

Grind the meat through a ¼" plate. Add the spices and water to the meat, then mix all together thoroughly. Either re–grind the mixture though a ⅛" plate, or run it through a food processor to emulsify. Stuff tightly into hog casing (38-42mm). Tie them into about 2" lengths with twine, being careful not to burst the casing. With the damper open, hang the sausages in the smoker to dry for one hour. Add ½ pan of dry smoke, then close the damper ¼ of the way. Raise the internal smoker temperature to 180°. When the knockwursts reach 135° internally, remove them from the smoker, then place them in 165° water until an internal temperature of 152° is achieved. Remove the sausages from the water. Cool, and then refrigerate. Knocks are a light brown color.

Knockwurst cooking in 165° water until reaching 152°

STOCKTON TWP PUBLIC LIBRARY
140 W. BENTON AVE.
STOCKTON, IL 61085

"Stuff the mixture into 6"– 8" synthetic casings"

N o t e s

....
....
....
....
....
....
....
....
....
....
....
....
....
....
....
....
....
....
....
....
....
....
....
....
....
....

BOLOGNA

5 Lbs. beef
5 Lbs. pork
6 Tb. salt
2 tsp. prague powder
1 Tb. paprika
1½ Tb. white pepper
2 tsp. nutmeg
1½ tsp. allspice
1 tsp. dry mustard
1 tsp. coriander
2 tsp. onion powder
½ Tb. garlic powder
2 C. ice water
2 C. powdered milk

Grind all of the meat through a $3/16$" plate.

Mix all of the spices and water together thoroughly, then blend together with the meat. Either re–grind the mixture through a $1/8$" plate, or run it through a food processor to emulsify.

Stuff the mixture into 6"– 8" synthetic casings, tying closed the finished end with twine. With the damper wide open, hang the bologna from smoke sticks and place them in the smoker for one hour.

Close the damper $1/4$ of the way, then add smoke. Raise the smoker temperature to 180°. Smoke until the bologna internal temperature reaches 152 °.

Remove the bologna from the smoker, then run them under cold water. Let the bologna cool down to 110°. Remove them from the cold water, then refrigerate.

Tip: Limpy **strongly** suggests ordering synthetic casings that are pre–tied at one end. They have a loop at the pre–tied end to slip the smoke stick through to hang in the smoker.

> "Place the mixture in the refrigerator for 4–5 hours"

N o t e s

....
....
....
....
....
....
....
....
....
....
....
....
....
....
....
....
....
....
....
....
....
....
....
....
....
....
....
....
....
....
....

SPANISH CHORIZO FIRE STICKS

10 Lbs. any combo of meat
6 Tb. salt
1 C. fermento
5 Tb. paprika
1 Tb. black pepper
1 Tb. white pepper
3 Tb. cayenne Pepper
1 tsp. crushed red chile
3 Tb. granulated garlic
2 tsp. prague powder
1 Tb. oregano
2 Tb. corn sugar (optional)
1 C. white vinegar
1 C. water

Grind the meat either through a $^3/_{16}$" or a $^1/_8$" plate.

Add all of the spices and water to the meat. Mix all together thoroughly, then place the mixture in the refrigerator for 4–5 hours.

Stuff the mixture into either 19mm. smoked collagen casings or into small hog casings. Link or tie into desired lengths.

Preheat the smoker to 140°. With the damper open, hang the links on smoke sticks and place the sausages into the preheated smoker. Smoke them for about two hours.

Without closing the damper, raise the smoker temperature to 180°. Leave the sausages in the smoker until their internal temperature reaches 150°.

Hang the sausages to cool, then refrigerate.

 Tip: Just because a sausage is smoked, doesn't mean it won't spoil. Refrigerate and/or freeze to avoid spoiling.

> **"Cook until the internal temperature of the sausages is 150°"**

N o t e s

....
....
....
....
....
....
....
....
....
....
....
....
....
....
....
....
....
....
....
....
....
....
....
....

PEPPERONI STICKS

5 Lbs. pork butt
5 Lbs. beef chuck
1½ Tb. garlic powder
7 Tb. salt
2 tsp. prague powder
2 Tb. sugar
3–4 Tb. paprika
1½ Tb. cayenne pepper
2 Tb. anise seed ground
1 tsp. allspice
1 tsp. dry mustard
2 C. nonfat powdered milk
½ C. fermento
2 Tb. corn sugar (optional)
2 C. water

Grind the pork through a ¹/₈" plate.

Grind the beef through a ³/₁₆" plate.

Mix all of the spices and water together, then add the mixture to the meat. Blend all together well. Stuff the mixture into hog casings.

Put the sausages onto smoke sticks and hang them in the smoker with the damper fully open until they are dry to the touch.

Close the damper ¹/₄ of the way. Raise the smoker temperature to 180°. Don't add smoke.

Cook until the internal temperature of the sausages is 150°.

After cooking, cool down the sausages, then refrigerate.

In all of these recipes that call for drying the sausage before smoking, leave the smoker door ajar to speed drying time.

"Salami will shrink if not cooled down right away"

N o t e s

. . . .
. . . .
. . . .
. . . .
. . . .
. . . .
. . . .
. . . .
. . . .
. . . .
. . . .
. . . .
. . . .
. . . .
. . . .
. . . .
. . . .
. . . .
. . . .
. . . .
. . . .
. . . .
. . . .
. . . .

BEEF SALAMI

10 Lbs. beef chuck
6 Tb. salt
1½ Tb. black pepper
1½ Tb. white pepper
2 Tb. paprika
1 Tb. ginger
1 Tb. cayenne pepper
1 Tb. garlic granulated
2 tsp. nutmeg
2 tsp. prague powder
½ tsp. coriander
4 Tb. corn sugar (optional)
1 Tb. sugar
2 C. water
2 C. nonfat powdered milk

Grind the meat through a $^3/_8$" plate. Mix together the water, spices, etc., then add the mixture to the meat. Re–grind the mixture through a $^1/_8$" plate. Stuff the re–ground mixture into 3"x 24" fibrous (synthetic) casings that have been soaking in a bath of $^2/_3$ parts water to $^1/_3$ part vinegar.

With the damper open **and** the smoker door ajar, hang the salami in the smoker until they are dry to the touch (approx. $^1/_2$ hour). This will prevent spotting.

After drying, close the damper $^1/_4$ of the way, then raise the smoker temperature to 180°. Add damp sawdust and smoke until the salami internal temperature reaches 152°. Remove them from the smoker, then cool in cold water until their internal temperature drops to 110°. Hang until dry, then refrigerate.

- Salami will shrink if not cooled down right away.
- Always use lean beef. Fatter beef will run and fill the inside of your casings.
- Before smoking, prick any air pockets in the casing with a pin to release the air.

"Stuff into 3" x 24" synthetic casings"

N o t e s

....
....
....
....
....
....
....
....
....
....
....
....
....
....
....
....
....
....
....
....
....
....
....
....
....
....
....
....
....
....
....
....
....
....
....

COTTO SALAMI

6 Lbs. beef chuck
4 Lbs. lean pork butt
2 C. ice water
6 Tb. salt
2 tsp. prague powder
4 Tb. corn sugar (optional)
2 Tb. black pepper
½ tsp. allspice
6 cloves garlic chopped
1 Tb. granulated garlic
2 Tb. cardamon
1 tsp. dry mustard
1½ Tb. **whole** black pepper
2 C. nonfat powdered milk

Grind the meat through a $^3/_8$" plate. Mix all of the spices and water together, then add to the meat. Re–grind the mixture through a $^1/_8$" plate. Stuff the mixture into 3" x 24" synthetic casings to make bologna–size salami (to slice for use in sandwiches), or for a standard–size cotto salami (good for use on crackers), stuff into 6"– 8" casings. With the damper wide open, hang the sausages in the smoker until they are dry to the touch. Then, close the damper $^1/_4$ turn. Add damp smoke, then raise the smoker temperature to 180°. Smoke until the internal sausage temperature reaches 152°. Remove, then cool under water until the internal sausage temperature is 110°. Hang to dry, then refrigerate.

Hickory Sawdust

Cotto Salami

Tip:

When smoking, Limpy uses 2 pans of moist sawdust. Adjust to your liking. Remove the smoke halfway through smoking, and finish off without the sawdust.

> *"Liver grinds easier if it's partially frozen"*

N o t e s

....
....
....
....
....
....
....
....
....
....
....
....
....
....
....
....
....
....
....
....
....
....
....
....
....
....
....
....

SMOKED LIVER SAUSAGE

4 Lbs. clean pork liver
4 Lbs. pork butt
2 Lbs. fatty bacon
6 Tb. salt
2 C. nonfat powdered milk
1 onion ground
1½ Tb. white pepper
½ tsp. marjoram
½ tsp. cloves ground
1 tsp. granulated garlic
½ tsp. ginger
½ tsp. nutmeg
½ tsp. sage
½ tsp. allspice
¼ tsp. coriander ground
2 tsp. prague powder
2 Tb. sugar
½ C. milk *or* turkey broth

Grind all of the meat through a ¹/₈" plate. Re–grind 2 to 3 more times, adding milk or broth in the **last** grind. Add all of the spices and powdered milk to the ground meat, then mix all together very well.

Take three 3" X 24" fibrous casings and cut each in half. Soak the casings in a bath of water and vinegar (²/₃ parts water to ¹/₃ part vinegar). Optionally, you can add a dash of liquid smoke. Stuff the mixture into these soaked casings. Prick any air pockets with a pin, then put the sausages into 165° preheated water. Cook until the sausage internal temperature reaches 152°. Remove and place in **ice cold** water until cool to the touch. Hang to dry. Then, place the sausages into a 140° preheated smoker for 2 hours with a pan of dry smoke. Remove the sausages from the smoker and run them under cold water for 10 minutes. Hang the sausages until dry, then refrigerate.

 Tip: Liver grinds easier if it's partially frozen.

> *"Smoke the sausages until their internal temp–erature reaches 152°"*

N o t e s

....
....
....
....
....
....
....
....
....
....
....
....
....
....
....
....
....
....
....
....
....
....
....
....

VENISON SALAMI

6 Lbs. venison
4 Lbs. pork butt
5 Tb. salt
2 C. nonfat powdered milk
1 Tb. white pepper
1 Tb. black pepper
1 Tb. cayenne pepper
2 tsp. prague powder
1 Tb. dry mustard
2 Tb. sugar
2 Tb. nutmeg
4 cloves garlic, chopped
1 Tb. granulated garlic
4 Tb. corn sugar (optional)
2 C. water

Grind the meat through a $3/8$" grinder plate. Mix together the spices, water, etc., then blend them together with the meat. Re-grind the mixture through $1/8$" plate.

Stuff the mixture into 3" x 24" fibrous (synthetic) casings that have been soaking in a bath of $2/3$ parts water to $1/3$ part vinegar with a dash of liquid smoke (optional). With the damper wide open, place the sausages into the smoker until they are dry to the touch.

Close the damper $1/4$ turn and add damp smoke. Raise the smoker temperature to 180°. Smoke the sausages until their internal temperature reaches 152°.

Venison Salami

Remove the sausages from the smoker, then run cold water over them until their internal temp–erature drops to 110°. Hang the salami until they are dry, then refrigerate.

> "Grind the fatter meat through a ³/₁₆" or a ¹/₈" plate"

N o t e s

....
....
....
....
....
....
....
....
....
....
....
....
....
....
....
....
....
....
....
....
....
....
....
....
....
....
....
....
....
....
....

VENISON SMOKIE LINKS

6 Lbs. venison
4 Lbs. fat pork butt
2 C. water
6 Tb. salt
1½ Tb. black pepper
1 Tb. white pepper
1 Tb. cayenne pepper
1 Tb. granulated onion
2 Tb. corn sugar (optional)
1 Tb. granulated garlic
2 tsp. prague powder
1½ tsp. nutmeg

Grind lean venison and pork through a ¹/₄" plate. Grind the fatter meat through a ³/₁₆" or a ¹/₈" plate. Mix the meats and other ingredients together and stuff the mixture into hog casings. Make into links of desired size.

Hang the links on smoke sticks and place them in the smoker for 1 hour with the damper open until they are dry. Close the damper ¹/₄ turn, and raise the smoker temperature to 180°. Smoke until the sausage internal temperature reaches 152°.

Run the links under cold water until they are cool. Hang the links until they are dry, then refrigerate. Limpy used to cool his sausage and salami in the sink, but as his batches became larger, the sink became too small. He made a rack outside where he could transfer his smoke sticks from the smoker directly to the rack. A sprinkler placed on a board underneath cools the sausage and salami down very quickly. When the sprinkler is turned off, you can leave the sausage in the rack to dry naturally.

Sausage cooling rack

"Jerky can be made from any cut of beef or venison"

N o t e s

....
....
....
....
....
....
....
....
....
....
....
....
....
....
....
....
....
....
....
....
....
....
....
....
....
....
....
....

"DOC'S" JERKY

Jerky can be made from any cut of beef or venison. Some people make jerky out of turkey, shark, ostrich or pork.

Limpy's grandfather "Doc" used to make jerky out of abalone, and cut a sliver off of the whole chunk with his pocket knife. As he recalls, it was pretty hard stuff!

Limpy's father makes the best jerky from the simplest method. Start with a good quality meat cut across the grain, with all of the sinews taken out. Add salt, pepper, and granulated garlic. Season heavily, like a good steak. Place in a bowl, then cover with a cloth and refrigerate for 24 hours.

Using a jerky box...

Limpy's father uses a jerky box, consisting of screen shelves, a heater fan on the bottom, and a hole cut in the top of the box. To ensure even drying, he pulls out the screen shelves and changes their position every so often, rotating the top shelf down to the bottom position and bringing the bottom shelf up, until the meat is jerked.

Limpy makes his in the same manner, but he cuts the meat *with* the grain for a chewier effect.
Somehow, Limpy's dad's always seems to be better.

Marinating your jerky...

Marinate all recipes for 24 hours. Following are a few recipes for 5 Lb. batches. Use good quality beef, elk or venison.

Jerky Marinade #1
5 tsp. salt
2 tsp. black pepper
½ C. brown sugar
1½ C. soy sauce
1 C. red wine vinegar

"You also can sun-dry the jerky on top of your roof"

N o t e s

....
....
....
....
....
....
....
....
....
....
....
....
....
....
....
....
....
....
....
....
....
....
....
....
....
....
....
....
....
....
....
....

Jerky Marinade #2
5 tsp. salt
2 tsp. black pepper
½ C. chili powder
2 tsp. cumin
2 Tb. granulated garlic
2 Tb. onion powder

Jerky Marinade #3
1 C. BBQ sauce
2 tsp. chili powder
2 tsp. cayenne pepper
2 Tb. liquid smoke
1½ Tb. Worcestershire sauce

Making your jerky...

You can build your own jerky screen rack (with a wooden frame), and dry your jerky in a *gas* oven using *only* the pilot light. Drying time depends on the thickness of your strips. A dehydrator works well also.

Alternatively, you can use a smoker. With the door ajar and the vent open, set the temperature at 115°–125°.

You also can sun–dry the jerky on top of your roof, making sure to encase it in a fine screen rack to keep the flies away. If you use this method, cover it with a sheet at night, so that fog or a cloudy night won't cause the meat to mildew.

If you are making a jerky box, use a heater fan on the bottom with a vent on the top.

If you have more than 2 shelves, rotate them top to bottom occasionally.

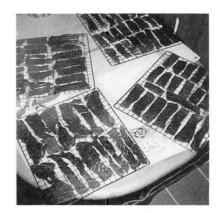

Homemade jerky

"Fish with high oil content smoke nicer"

N o t e s

. . . .
. . . .
. . . .
. . . .
. . . .
. . . .
. . . .
. . . .
. . . .
. . . .
. . . .
. . . .
. . . .
. . . .
. . . .
. . . .
. . . .
. . . .
. . . .
. . . .
. . . .
. . . .
. . . .

SMOKED SALMON

Fillet the salmon

On a pan, place the fillets side–by–side with the skin side down.

Mix together:
- 1 C. brown sugar
- ½ C. white sugar
- ½ C. salt

Rub the mixture over the fillets and cover them. Then, place the fillets in the refrigerator for 24 hours. After 24 hours, remove them and wash them gently under cold water.

With the damper open, place them on a rack in the smoker until they are dry to the touch. As an option, you can lay a handmade rack across your smoke sticks. After drying, close the damper ¼ turn and raise the temperature to 165°, while adding smoke. You can use apple and alder mix, or hickory and apple mix. Smoke until the salmon temperature is 140°. Remove and cool.

Whole fresh trout can be brined in the same way. Whole bonita, mackerel, tuna, and barracuda can also be brined and smoked. Normally, fish with high oil content smoke nicer because they don't dry out. Halibut, sea bass, and shark tend to toughen up due to the tight grain and lack of oil in the meat.

Smoked Salmon

 Tip: Smoke a little on the under–cooked side, so that the fish won't dry out.

"Add potatoes, carrots, and cabbage about 45 minutes before the meat will be done"

N o t e s

....
....
....
....
....
....
....
....
....
....
....
....
....
....
....
....
....
....
....
....
....
....
....
....
....

Pickled Recipes

CORNED BEEF OR CORNED TONGUE

BRINE:
5 qt. ice water
¾ Lb. salt
3 oz. sugar
3 oz. prague powder
½ C. pickling spices
8 cloves garlic, crushed *or* 3 Tb. garlic juice

Using a brine pump, inject the solution all around the sides, top and bottom of the meat.

Put the meat in a lugger or in a non–aluminum bowl.

Add the spices and completely cover the meat with leftover brine for 4 or 5 days.

Remove the meat from the brine and place it into a large pot of water. After bringing the water to a boil, reduce heat and simmer until the meat is fork tender (about 2 hours).

Add potatoes, carrots, and cabbage about 45 minutes before the meat will be done.

Use a brine pump to pump the meat with the brine solution

"Pour the solution over hot meats or whatever you are pickling"

N o t e s

....
....
....
....
....
....
....
....
....
....
....
....
....
....
....
....
....
....
....
....
....
....
....
....
....
....
....
....
....
....
....
....

VINEGAR PICKLE BRINE

2 C. white vinegar
1 onion, sliced
1 bay leaf
1 Tb. sugar
2 cloves garlic and 1 whole cayenne pepper, dried (to be added later).

Bring the vinegar, onion and bay leaf to a boil, then lower heat.

Simmer for 20 minutes, then strain out the bay leaf and onion.

Add $1^1/_2$ C. hot water and the sugar.

Pour the solution over hot meats or whatever you are pickling. Then, add the garlic and cayenne pepper. Allow to cool completely, then jar and refrigerate for 4 or 5 days.

Other items that you can pickle using this brine solution:

    1. Pork hocks and shanks
    2. Pork neck bones
    3. Hardboiled eggs (peeled)
    4. Beets (cooked and peeled)
    5. Onions, celery, carrots, peppers, bell peppers, Ortega chiles (precooked)

Prepare as instructed above.

N o t e s

....
....
....
....
....
....
....
....
....
....
....
....
....
....
....
....
....
....
....
....
....
....
....
....
....
....
....
....
....

Limpy's Favorite Recipes

CHILE VERDE (PORK)

6 Lbs. pork, cut into 1" cubes
1 bell pepper
6 cloves garlic, diced
4 large cans whole tomatoes
3 large cans whole green chiles
3 Jalapeño chiles (optional)
1 bunch cilantro, chopped
1 bunch parsley, chopped
1 Tb. sugar
½ tsp. ground cloves
2 Tb. ground cumin
3 C. Burgundy wine
Salt, pepper

Season the meat with salt and pepper.

In a dutch oven or a large pot, brown the meat in olive oil (about 2–3 Tb.).

Add the garlic and the rest of the ingredients.

Cover, then bring to a boil.

Remove from the stove and place into a preheated 300° oven for approx. 3 hours, stirring occasionally.

Serve with corn or flour tortillas.

 Tip: All stews, chiles and soups need to be re-seasoned from time to time to your liking.

> "Mix all together and place into a loaf pan to bake"

N o t e s

....
....
....
....
....
....
....
....
....
....
....
....
....
....
....
....
....
....
....
....
....
....
....
....
....
....

MEATLOAF

1½ Lbs. ground venison
1½ Lbs. ground pork
Salt, pepper, and garlic (desired amount)
1 small onion, diced
2 eggs
2 Tb. Worcestershire sauce
½ C. chopped black olives
½ C. chopped green chiles (optional)
1 C. seasoned Italian bread crumbs
milk to mix

Mix all together and place into a loaf pan to bake. If you prefer, cover with slices of your own cured bacon, or store–bought bacon.

Bake at 350° for 1 hour and 15 minutes.
Serve with mashed potatoes.

As an option, you can substitute turkey or chicken for the venison (prepare as instructed above). Adding a dash of chicken broth to the mix will make this a mild meat loaf.

 Tip: This meatloaf is also great in a sandwich with red onion slices and spicy mustard served on Shepherd's bread.

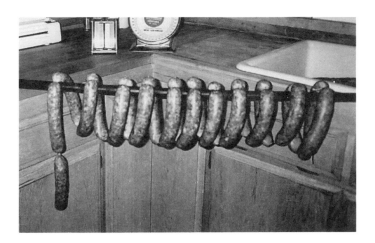

Sausages hanging on a smoke stick

"Bake in a preheated 350° oven for approx. 2 hours"

N o t e s

....
....
....
....
....
....
....
....
....
....
....
....
....
....
....
....
....
....
....
....
....
....
....
....
....
....
....
....

VENISON STEW

2 Lbs. or so venison, cut into chunks or 1" cubes
4 potatoes, cut into 1" pieces
6 large carrots, cut
3 or 4 stalks of celery, cut
1 handful of small mushrooms
2 medium onions, coarsely cut
1 C. frozen peas
Green beans (optional)
Zucchini (optional)
Broth, either beef or turkey
1 Tb. kitchen boquet, or any beef concentrate
2 bay leaves
2 Tb. Worcestershire sauce
2–3 Tb. olive oil

In a large dutch oven or any heavy pot, heat the olive oil. Brown the onion in the olive oil. Remove the onion, then set it aside.

Mix together the salt, pepper, flour and garlic powder. Add the mixture to the meat. Brown in the pot, adding more oil if needed. Add the onion, and the rest of the ingredients to the pot, or dutch oven. Cover with broth about two inches over.

Bring to a boil, then cover. Remove from the stove burner, and bake in a preheated 350° oven for approx. 2 hours, stirring the stew now and then.

If you like a thicker stew, add a little flour until the desired thickness is obtained.

Make drop biscuits to serve with the stew (see the recipe on page 82).

 Tip: So that your flour won't lump when adding it to the stew, dissolve it in a little liquid first.

> "To coat the meat, dip it in flour or corn starch"

N o t e s

....
....
....
....
....
....
....
....
....
....
....
....
....
....
....
....
....
....
....
....
....
....
....
....
....
....
....
....

VENISON PAN-FRIED STEAK (chicken fried steak)

Take your venison loin or boneless round meat, and slice it thin. Pound the meat on both sides.

On both sides of the meat, put salt, pepper, season salt, or granulated garlic.

Then, to coat the meat, dip it in flour or corn starch.

Heat olive oil in a hot skillet, then add the meat. Brown it until blood comes through. Turn the meat over and brown on the other side.

Remove the meat and place it on a plate.

Repeat the above steps until all of the meat is done.

If you like, you can return the meat to the skillet, and add a shot of wine or sherry to steep.

Cover and reduce heat for a minute or so.
Remove, and serve with rice or mashed potatoes.

• If you like, you can make gravy out of the drippings in the pan.

• When you cut up your deer, put aside pieces of meat that are to nice to grind, and use these pieces for this recipe. Leave about one pound pieces whole to freeze, so that you can slice them later.

• Pork can be fixed in the same way as pan-fried venison. However, it comes out tasting like the veal that you would find served in a restaurant.

N o t e s

....
....
....
....
....
....
....
....
....
....
....
....
....
....
....
....
....
....
....
....
....
....
....
....
....
....
....
....
....

CHILE BEANS

3 cups favorite dry beans (or mixed variety), soaked over night
1 large onion, chopped
6 cloves garlic, chopped
Salt
Black pepper
Red pepper
1 Tb. oregano
1 Tb. cumin
4 Tb. chile powder
1½ Lbs. ground venison, pork, or beef
28 oz. can whole tomatoes
14 oz. can whole tomatoes
14 oz. can tomato paste
1 small can tomato sauce

In a large pot, brown the meat in about 2 Tb. olive oil.

Drain the beans (see tip on page 68).

Mix in the spices and the tomato sauces.

Add enough water or broth to cover an inch over the mixture.

Bring to a boil.

Reduce heat, cover with a lid and simmer for 3 hours until it is the desired thickness.

Serve with corn bread.

These chile beans are great the next day for breakfast. Start with a couple of scrambled eggs and medium grated sheese. In tortillas, add the beans, scrambled eggs and the cheese. Roll up the tortillas and heat until the cheese is melted. What a breakfast!

"Cook down about 3 hours until thick"

N o t e s

....
....
....
....
....
....
....
....
....
....
....
....
....
....
....
....
....
....
....
....
....
....
....
....
....
....
....
....

LEFT OVER BEANS (MEAT OR SAUSAGE)

3 Lbs. favorite dry beans, soaked over night
2–3 Lbs. leftover meat (bar–b–que'd is best)
2 white onions, chopped
1 Lb. bacon, cubed
6 cloves garlic, chopped
8 C. choice of either turkey broth, beef broth, **or** water
2 Tb. Worcestershire sauce
1 Tb. black pepper
Salt to taste
½ tsp. seasoned pepper
1 palmful of parsley flakes

Drain the beans.

Brown the bacon in a large pan.

Remove the bacon, then add the onion and garlic. Brown them in the bacon grease.

Add the meat and bacon, and all of the remaining ingredients.

Add water or your favorite broth to cover an inch above the mixture.

Bring to a boil.

Reduce heat, simmer, and cook down about 3 hours until thick.

Serve with french bread or warm tortillas.

 Tip:

If you don't have time to soak dry beans overnight, go ahead and use canned beans that have been well drained. Use as many cans that you think you'll need for your servings. This applies to all bean recipes.

"Place into the oven for 1 hour at 375°"

N o t e s

. . . .
. . . .
. . . .
. . . .
. . . .
. . . .
. . . .
. . . .
. . . .
. . . .
. . . .
. . . .
. . . .
. . . .
. . . .
. . . .
. . . .
. . . .
. . . .
. . . .
. . . .

QUICK BEAN AND SMOKED SAUSAGE CASEROLE

2 16 oz. cans pork & beans in tomato sauce
1 bell pepper, chopped
1 onion, chopped
2 Tb. yellow mustard
½ C. ketchup
1½ Lbs. smoked Polish sausage, hot links or hot dogs.

Cut the sausage into ¾" chunks.

Add all of the ingredients, mixing them together well.

Cover, then place into the oven for 1 hour at 375°.

Serve with rice.

Your homemade Polish sausage or hot dogs are the best to use. They are not mushy, like the store-bought ones. Also, they have less fat.

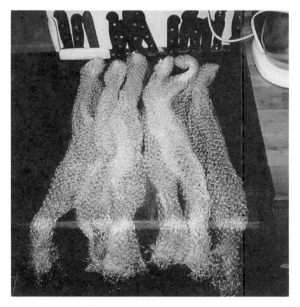

Ham netting, which can also be used to hang poultry from the smoke stick

N o t e s

....
....
....
....
....
....
....
....
....
....
....
....
....
....
....
....
....
....
....
....
....
....
....
....
....
....
....
....
....

BEANS WITH TURKEY

Smoked turkey meat (see tip below)
1 Lb. small white navy beans
1 onion
2 cloves garlic, chopped
1 Tb. Worcestershire sauce
1 palmful of parsley flakes
Turkey broth (to cover)
Salt and pepper
1 bay leaf (optional)

Soak the beans over night (see tip on page 68).

Drain the beans.

Put the beans, chopped turkey, onion, etc. into a pot.

Cover the ingredients 2" above with broth.

Bring to a boil.

Simmer 3 or more hours until thick, removing any bones as you stir.

Tip: For an alternative, after you smoke a turkey use the drumsticks, wings, or carcass for this recipe in place of traditional ham hocks. This utilizes the pieces that are most wasteful.

"Refrigerate until the potato salad sets up and the flavors blend. About 3 hours should do it"

N o t e s

....
....
....
....
....
....
....
....
....
....
....
....
....
....
....
....
....
....
....
....
....
....

POTATO SALAD

4 large potatoes
½ C. mayonnaise
1 Tb. yellow mustard
1 small bunch green onions, diced
2 stalks celery, chopped
Salt and pepper to taste

Peel and boil the potatoes until they are cooked but still slightly firm. Cool, then cut them into chunks and place them into a large bowl.

Add the mayonnaise, mustard, chopped celery and diced green onions (refer to tips, bottom of page). Mix them together thoroughly, then add salt and pepper to taste. Feel free to add more mayonnaise or mustard according to your taste.

Some people like a splash of wine vinegar in their salad.

Refrigerate until the potato salad sets up and the flavors blend. About 3 hours should do it.

Re–taste and re–season, if needed.

• If you are going to make this the day before, hold off on the onion until the day that you serve it. The set up onion taste might become too strong.

• You can also bake the potatoes if you wish. After baking, cut them in half lengthwise and remove the cooked potato from the skins. Save the skins for the recipe on the following page.

> "Sprinkle the empty potato skins with grated cheese and bacon"

N o t e s

. . . .
. . . .
. . . .
. . . .
. . . .
. . . .
. . . .
. . . .
. . . .
. . . .
. . . .
. . . .
. . . .
. . . .
. . . .
. . . .
. . . .

POTATO SKINS

If you baked the potatoes to make your potato salad, here is a recipe where you can use your saved potato skins.

Empty potato skins
½ Lb. bacon
Medium cheddar cheese, grated
Ranch dressing

Dice and fry the bacon until crisp.

Grate enough cheese that you feel you'll need according to how many empty potato skins that you have.

For a pre - bar–b–que treat, dust the empty potato skins with a sprinkle of grated cheese and bacon.

Put the skins on a baking dish and place the baking dish into the oven and bake at 350° until the cheese is melted.

Serve on a plate with ranch dressing for dipping.

Lugger and stainless steel bowls for sausage making

> *"The salad will set up and the flavors will blend after a few hours in the refrigerator"*

N o t e s

. . . .
. . . .
. . . .
. . . .
. . . .
. . . .
. . . .
. . . .
. . . .
. . . .
. . . .
. . . .
. . . .
. . . .
. . . .
. . . .
. . . .
. . . .
. . . .
. . . .
. . . .
. . . .
. . . .
. . . .
. . . .

MACARONI SALAD

1 package elbow macaroni
½ can black olives
½ small bunch green onions
2 stalks celery
1 Tb. yellow mustard
½ C. mayonnaise
Salt and pepper to taste
1 can drained tuna (optional)

Cook the macaroni, following the instructions on the package, then cool.

Put the cooled macaroni in a large bowl, then add to it the $^1/_2$ can of chopped olives. Dice the celery and onion and add them to the bowl. Mix all together thoroughly.

Add the mayonnaise and mustard, salt and pepper. Mix all together and taste.

Usually the salad will set up and the flavors will blend after a few hours in the refrigerator. Re–taste before serving. Add more mayonnaise if needed.

To add color, you can sprinkle the top of the salad with diced green onion ends and sliced hard boiled eggs.

Refrigerate until you are ready to serve.

 Tip:

If you make the salad a day in advance of when you serve it, hold off on adding all of the onions until immediately before you are ready to serve. The onion taste might become too strong if you let it stand overnight.

> *"Too much mayonnaise will make your egg filling too loose"*

N o t e s

....
....
....
....
....
....
....
....
....
....
....
....
....
....
....
....
....
....
....
....
....
....
....
....
....

LIMPY'S DEVILED EGGS

6 hard boiled eggs
$1/3$ C. mayonnaise
1½ TB. yellow mustard
1 tsp. salt
½ tsp. white pepper
¼ tsp. cayenne pepper

Place the eggs in a pot and cover them with water. Bring them to a rolling boil, then cover the pot for 10 minutes. Remove the eggs from the stove and run them under cold water for 4 or 5 minutes. This prevents the eggs from continuing to cook, and also prevents the yolks from turning gray. Refrigerate until the eggs are cold. The eggs will be easy to crack and peel now. Make sure that all the shells are peeled off completely by running the eggs under cold water as you peel them. Nothing is worse than an egg shell in your finished product.

Cut the eggs in half lengthwise, and scoop the yolks into a bowl. Set the cooked egg whites aside. With a fork, mash the yolks until they are workable. Then add the mayonnaise, half of your mustard, salt, pepper and cayenne powder. Mix all of the ingredients together until you get the smooth consistency that you like. Taste the egg mixture. Add the remaining mustard in small amounts until you get the taste that you like. It's much easier to add more mustard to taste than it is to add mayonnaise to cover up the mustard if you added too much. Also, too much mayonnaise will make your egg filling too loose.

When you have acquired the taste and texture that suits you, take a spoon and spoon the filling back into the empty halved eggs whites.

If you like, you may sprinkle the tops of your finished product with parsley flakes or paprika. Refrigerate until you are ready to serve.

"Start at the rounded end of the cabbage and shred all the way to the end"

N o t e s

....
....
....
....
....
....
....
....
....
....
....
....
....
....
....
....
....
....
....
....
....
....
....
....
....

COLE SLAW

1 head of green cabbage
¼ to ½ grated brown or white onion
1 large carrot
2 stalks celery
¼ C. red wine vinegar
½ C. mayonnaise
Salt and pepper to taste

Wash and core the cabbage and cut it in half with a sharp knife. Start at the rounded end of the cabbage and shred all the way to the end.

Put the shredded cabbage in a large bowl.

Dice the celery, then add it to the cabbage.

Mix together the cabbage, onion, celery, and carrot together. Add the mayonnaise and **half** of the amount of wine vinegar.

Thoroughly mix everything together, then add salt and pepper to taste.

When you have the taste you like, refrigerate until you are ready to serve.

• If you need more vinegar, add it sparingly. This also applies to adding more mayonnaise.

• Limpy likes to grate the carrot and onion

"For a real thick sauce, add a small amount of corn starch"

N o t e s

. . . .
. . . .
. . . .
. . . .
. . . .
. . . .
. . . .
. . . .
. . . .
. . . .
. . . .
. . . .
. . . .
. . . .
. . . .
. . . .
. . . .
. . . .
. . . .
. . . .
. . . .
. . . .
. . . .

Toppings

QUICK AND EASY B.B.Q. SAUCE

1 C. strong brewed black coffee
1½ C. brown sugar
½ onion, diced
1¼ C. ketchup
1 Tb. dry mustard
2 Tb. Balsamic or cider vinegar
2 Tb. Worcestershire sauce
1 tsp. salt
Dash pepper

Mix all ingredients in a sauce pan.
Bring to a boil.
Stir and reduce heat.
Simmer for ½ hour.
If you like a real thick sauce, add a small amount of pre-dissolved corn starch.

KNOCKWURST OR HOT DOG TOPPING

½ C. ketchup
1 Tb. good pickle relish
2 Tb. yellow mustard
1 small red onion, chopped

Mix all of the ingredients together.
Taste, then readjust to your liking.
Take your knockwurst or ¼ Lb. hot dog and slice it in half. You will now have two short pieces.
Split each short piece lengthwise (butterfly) and place one split piece on a hamburger bun.
The knockwursts are almost too big for a hot dog bun!!
Spread your new topping on top.

N o t e s

....
....
....
....
....
....
....
....
....
....
....
....
....
....
....
....
....
....
....
....
....
....
....
....
....
....
....
....
....
....
....
....

TASTY–EASY HOT DOG RELISH

Now that you have the perfect hot dog in a bun, top it off with this great relish.

12 large cucumbers, peeled
4 onions
5 green bell peppers
1 red bell pepper
4 tsp. celery seed
5 tsp. whole mustard seed
1 tsp. salt
½ tsp. cloves, ground
1¼ Tb. tumeric
3½ cups sugar
3½ cups cider vinegar
6–8 quart stainless steel pot (**not** aluminum)

Take the first four vegetables, and either grind them using a $^3/_{16}$" plate, or chop them finely. Place them into a large pot. Make sure you are using a kettle or pot that is **not** aluminum. Add the remaining ingredients. Bring to a boil. Stir constantly so as not to burn. Reduce heat, and simmer about 3 hours with the pot uncovered. Stir occasionally until the mixture thickens.

Ladle the relish into **sterile** pint jars ($^1/_2$" from the rim). Run a nonmetallic spatula or the like around the inside of the jar to remove any air pockets. In a canning pot (it comes with a special bottom rack to hold your canning jars), submerge the filled jars that have been sealed with sterile lids completely in water. The water should cover the jars. Bring to a boil, then cover the pot with a lid. Now set the timer for 15 minutes. Remove the jars, then let them cool on thick towels or on a wooden cutting board. This helps prevent the jars from cracking, which could happen if they are set onto a cold kitchen counter top. Sealed jars will last about a year or so. Refrigerate the jars that don't seal tight, and use them first.

Makes about 6 pints.

N o t e s

· ·
· ·
· ·
· ·
· ·
· ·
· ·
· ·
· ·
· ·
· ·
· ·
· ·
· ·
· ·
· ·
· ·
· ·
· ·
· ·
· ·
· ·
· ·
· ·

HOMEMADE SALSA

4 28 oz. cans whole tomatoes
2 cans (largest) whole chiles
3 red onions, chopped
1 bunch cilantro
1 bunch parsley
2–3 Tb. celery seed
Salt
Pepper
Juice from 1 lemon
3 cloves garlic
Olive oil to taste
Red wine vinegar to taste
2 Tb. Worcestershire sauce
1 Tb. sugar
1 large can tomato sauce

Chop everything by hand.

Mix all together completely.

Taste, then readjust to your liking.

Taste again the next day and readjust to your liking.

Homemade Salsa

*"Let the dough rise
for 45 minutes"*

N o t e s

....
....
....
....
....
....
....
....
....
....
....
....
....
....
....
....
....
....
....
....
....
....
....
....
....
....
....
....
....
....
....

EASY PIZZA DOUGH

After years of searching to make the perfect pizza crust, this is as close as Limpy has come!

1 package rapid rise yeast
1 Tb. malt or sugar
2 Tb. shortening
1 Tb. salt
3½ C. flour
½ C. corn meal (mix with the flour)
1½ C. warm water (110°)

Add ½ cup warm water to the yeast and malt to activate. If yeast is active, add remaining warm water. Add the remaining ingredients.

Knead the dough until it is soft and smooth. Cover in a bowl. Let the dough rise for 45 minutes or until it has doubled. Pour out onto a pan. Let the dough rest for 10 minutes until it is workable.

Spread the dough in the pan. Prick the dough all over with a fork. Add sauce, Parmesan cheese, salt, pepper, favorite cheese, and favorite toppings.

Place the pizza into a cold oven on the lowest rack. Heat to 500°, and let bake for 18 minutes. Check at 15 minutes. The cheese should be melted and bubbly.

Better than a Pizzeria!

Be careful not to cook for too long, as the cheese will burn. All of your favorite sausages (breakfast, Italian, etc.) or Canadian bacon will go well on this dough.

"Mix well, go for it!!!"

N o t e s

....
....
....
....
....
....
....
....
....
....
....
....
....
....
....
....
....
....
....
....
....
....
....
....
....
....
....
....
....
....
....
....
....
....
....
....

FAVORITE PIZZA SAUCE

1 can tomato puree
½ tsp. oregano
½ tsp. basil
½ tsp. black pepper
¼ tsp. granulated garlic
¼ tsp. onion powder
2 Tb. Parmesan cheese
½ tsp. salt

Mix well, go for it!!!

This sauce doesn't require simmering on the stove before using it. It is made cold.

When people stop by unexpectedly, or there is a "big game" on T.V., this sauce can be whipped up easily to make a quick snack.

In place of pizza, you can spread this sauce on sliced French rolls, French bread or English muffins.

Top your chosen bread with cheese, sliced olives, sausage, onion, etc. and place in the broiler to heat and melt the cheese.

"Bake for 25 minutes, or until a tooth pick comes out clean when removed"

N o t e s

LIGHT & FLUFFY CORN BREAD

8 Tb. butter (or bacon drippings)
1 C. buttermilk
¾ C. whole milk
1½ C. flour
1½ C. yellow corn meal
3½ Tb. sugar
4 tsp. baking powder
½ tsp. baking soda
1 tsp. salt
2 eggs
1 C. corn kernels (fresh or frozen)
9"x13" pan or cast iron skillet

Mix the dry ingredients together.

In a separate bowl, mix together the eggs, milk and buttermilk.

Incorporate the liquid mixture together with the dry ingredients.

Then, add the corn.

Melt butter in a **hot** pan.

Add the mixture to the melted butter. Spread onto the pan, and place into a preheated 425° oven.

Bake for 25 minutes, or until a tooth pick comes out clean when removed.

Tip: If you want to zip up this recipe, add a small diced bell pepper.

"Drop the mix from a spoon onto an un-greased cookie sheet"

N o t e s

....
....
....
....
....
....
....
....
....
....
....

EASY BAKING POWDER BISCUITS

2½ C. flour
1 Tb. baking powder
1½ tsp. salt
$^1/_3$ C. vegetable oil
$^3/_4$ C. buttermilk or regular milk

Mix all together well and drop the mix from a spoon onto an ungreased cookie sheet.

Bake for about 12–15 minutes in a preheated 475° oven.

These biscuits are great for breakfast. Just like in the restaurants, you can make gravy to serve with the biscuits (see below).

Fry up some sausage, bacon or ham in a pan, then remove. To the drippings, add a couple of Tb. flour, a dash of milk, and some butter until you get the gravy to your desired thickness.

The gravy can be spooned over the biscuits, or sopped up after.

Of course, you can't rule out the old standards, honey or jam!

 Tip: For a smoother biscuit, you can add a little more flour and roll out the dough, using a biscuit cutter to cut out the biscuits.

Taking care of your own game, from skinning, gutting, processing, sausage making, etc. is very rewarding. You will be amazed at all of the meat, sausage, and favorite recipes that come from your initial game.

If you should make a mistake, i.e, the sausage is too lean or too fat, the nice thing is that you can eat your mistakes.

Just remember to keep the meat as clean and cold as you can, from the time your trophy animal is bagged, until your last bit of ground meat or sausage is finished.

Keep your work area and equipment as sterile as possible.

These references will be handy when you need supplies or help with information.

SOURCES FOR SAUSAGE MAKING:

Koch Supplies, Inc.
1411 W. 29th St.
Kansas City, MO 64108

California Butcher Supply
451 Los Coches St.
P.O. Box 360801
Milpitas, CA 95036

Out of Jackies Smoke House
The Outback Ranch, Inc. Box 9
Millville, CA 96062

Jafco Products
(Paper and Packaging Materials, Party Supplies)
110 Easy Street
Buellton, CA 93427
phone: (805) 688-5104
fax: (805) 688-1261

Sausage Maker
1500 Clinton St. #123
Buffalo, NY 14206

Hobart Equipment
2500 - A Knoll Dr.
Ventura, CA 93003
phone: (805) 658-1533
fax: (805) 658-2504

South Bay Abrams
P.O. Box 2118
Huntington Beach, CA 92647-0118